YOUR KNOWLEDGE HAS VALUE

AF150927

- We will publish your bachelor's and
  master's thesis, essays and papers

- Your own eBook and book -
  sold worldwide in all relevant shops

- Earn money with each sale

Upload your text at www.GRIN.com
and publish for free

GRIN

Roman Huditsch

SVG (Scalable Vector Graphics) - Overview about the possibilities and advantages as well as the current implementations of the new XML-based standard for Web graphics

GRIN Publishing

Bibliographic information published by the German National Library:

The German National Library lists this publication in the National Bibliography; detailed bibliographic data are available on the Internet at http://dnb.dnb.de .

This book is copyright material and must not be copied, reproduced, transferred, distributed, leased, licensed or publicly performed or used in any way except as specifically permitted in writing by the publishers, as allowed under the terms and conditions under which it was purchased or as strictly permitted by applicable copyright law. Any unauthorized distribution or use of this text may be a direct infringement of the author s and publisher s rights and those responsible may be liable in law accordingly.

Imprint:

Copyright © 2002 GRIN Verlag, Open Publishing GmbH
Print and binding: Books on Demand GmbH, Norderstedt Germany
ISBN: 978-3-656-21955-2

This book at GRIN:

http://www.grin.com/en/e-book/195495/svg-scalable-vector-graphics-overview-about-the-possibilities-and-advantages

GRIN - Your knowledge has value

Since its foundation in 1998, GRIN has specialized in publishing academic texts by students, college teachers and other academics as e-book and printed book. The website www.grin.com is an ideal platform for presenting term papers, final papers, scientific essays, dissertations and specialist books.

Visit us on the internet:

http://www.grin.com/

http://www.facebook.com/grincom

http://www.twitter.com/grin_com

SVG (Scalable Vector Graphics)

By Roman Huditsch

Overview about the possibilities and advantages as well as the current implementations of the new XML- based standard for Web graphics

Fachenglisch III – 6th Semester

Seminar Paper

Fachhochschul-Studiengang Informationsberufe

June 2002

Legal Notice:

The present seminar paper is Copyright © 2002 by Roman Huditsch. It may be copied, posted and/or distributed, in any way, shape, or form, in any print, magnetic, electronic, visual or optical mediums, for personal use only. It may therefore not be sold or used for commercial profit in any form or fashion without the explicit permission of the author. The content of the seminar paper may not be modified in any way without informing the originator.

Abstract

This seminar paper was written in the summer semester 2002 during an English course, which was taught by Veronica Dal- Bianco B.Sc. RSA Dip. at the Fachhochschulstudiengang Informationsberufe in Eisenstadt, Austria.

It is my intention to provide the interested reader with a complete and detailed overview of the new Web standard for vector graphics, SVG, which is the acronym for "Scalable Vector Graphics". In the present paper important milestones in the long lasting development process of SVG are mentioned, as well as it states the numerous advantages that result from the useage of this new XML- based standard. Furthermore, an insight into the current status and availability of the most popular and interesting SVG implementations should be delivered.

I might make use of some termini technici which are widely common in the XML and markup community, but may be unknown to readers new to this topic. Such terms can be found in a glossary contained in the appendix.

Table of Contents

1 Introduction

SVG is the new XML-based standard for Web graphics and is the acronym for "Scalable Vector Graphics". It allows Web designers and developers to easily create highly interactive two-dimensial vector graphics, on which they can apply a wide range of filter effects and animations. In the subsequent chapters I will provide more information about the development process of SVG, its main concepts and current implementations.

1.1 Current Status of SVG

The first public working draft for SVG was published on 2nd February 1999 by the World Wide Web consortium (W3C), which is an organisation of about 500 members that has already "developed more than 35 technical specifications for the Web's infrastructure" (W3C, 1999) since it was created in October 1994. This draft already contains information about the SVG's main goals and purposes. Since this point of time new more elaborated drafts have been released every two months on the average.

It lasted two and a half years since SVG finally reached the status of a W3C Recommendation on the 4th September 2001. In its current form, the Recommendation consists of 617 pages divided in 23 chapters and is edited by Jon Ferraiolo, who is Senior Computer Scientist at Adobe Systems Inc.

Although the SVG Recommendation was not written for ordinary users but for technical implementors, due to numerous examples it is not difficult to understand. According to the information provided at the W3C site for SVG work has already continued on the modular SVG 1.1[1] and on the "Mobile SVG profiles"[2] specification. For further information about the ongoing development process please check the related W3C sites.

---

[1] The recent working draft for SVG 1.1 can be found at
http://www.w3.org/TR/SVG11/

[2] More information about "Moblie SVG profiles" are located at
http://www.w3.org/TR/SVGMobile/

1.2   Primary Concepts

Before describing the meaning of the components "scalable" "vector" and "graphics", I want to provide you with the W3C's definition of SVG:

> *"SVG is a language for describing two-dimensional graphics in XML. SVG allows for three types of graphic objects: vector graphic shapes (e.g., paths consisting of straight lines and curves), images and text.*
>
> *[...]*
>
> *Text can be in any XML namespace suitable to the appplication, which enhances searchability and accessibility of the SVG graphics. The feature set includes nested transformations, clipping paths, alpha masks, filter effects, template objects and extensibility.*
>
> *SVG drawings can be dynamic and interactive. The Document Object Model (DOM) for SVG, which includes the full XML DOM, allows for straightforward and efficient vector graphics animation via scripting. ...*
>
> (2001)

As you can see from the definition above, SVG offers a wide range of possible applications. SVG is for example perfectly qualified to be used for creating complete Web sites[3] or for displaying quantitative data stored in XML files, which might be provided by a native XML database (e.g. Software AG's Tamino). This is just a short abstract of all the imaginable applications for SVG. If you are searching for more sophisticated examples, you can find them at Adobe's "SVG Zone"[4].

As I have already stated before, SVG stands for "Scalable Vector Graphics" and is a subset of XML for representing vector graphics with pure ASCII code. This brings the advantage of XML's openness, transportability and interoperability. Since SVG is an XML application, it can be used stand-alone or embedded in other subsets of XML like for example XHTML or MathML[5].

---

[3] if you want to take a look at my personal homepage completly created with SVG, you can find it at http://huditsch.piranho.com/

[4] http://www.adobe.com/SVG/

[5] MathML is an XML application designed for representing mathematical functions and equations

According to the W3C being scalable in terms of graphics means not being limited to a single, prescribed pixel size. Thus you can increase or decrease your graphic uniformly without losing quality. SVG furthermore offers the possibility to reuse already written code within the same graphic or to reference it inside other SVG graphics allowing complex illustrations to be built up in many different parts.

Due to the fact that SVG is a vector format, the graphic itself is made up of curves, lines and other mathematical shapes. Hence there is no need to store information about every single pixel of the graphic, but to save details about the mathematical functions to describe its basic shapes.

1.3 SVG's Benefits

Beside the already mentioned benefits, SVG can offer many other conveniences as well. The following markup code should illustrate the clear and plain structure of a typical SVG graphic:

```
<?xml version="1.0" standalone="no"?>
<!—The following code line has to be implemented to anounce a SVG
     graphic -->
<!DOCTYPE svg PUBLIC "-//W3C//DTD SVG 20010904//EN"
"http://www.w3.org/TR/2001/REC-SVG-20010904/DTD/svg10.dtd">
<svg width="800" height="600" xmlns="http://www.w3.org/2000/svg">
     <desc>Some basic shapes in SVG</desc>
     <!-- Definition for a typicall rectangle -->
     <rect x="400" y="100" width="400" height="200" fill="yellow"
          stroke="navy" stroke-width="10" />
     <!-- Here comes a red circle with a blue outline -->
     <circle cx="600" cy="200" r="100" fill="red" stroke="blue"
          stroke-width="10" />
     <!-- A polygon is simple to draw, too -->
     <polygon fill="lime" stroke="blue" stroke-width="10"
          points="850,75  958,137.5 958,262.5 850,325 742,262.6
          742,137.5" />
</svg>
```

Image 1: SVG example source code

Since the structure of SVG is that simple and human- readable, it can be learned very quickly. As I stated in the previous chapter, SVG provides all known advantages of common vector graphics like for example wmf (Windows-Meta-File format) or cgm (Computer Grafics Metafile). Beside the fact that compared to raster-formats like JPG or PNG SVG files are very small in size, you can zoom in or zoom out your grafic without losing quality.

One of the biggest advantages of SVG is its ability to apply client-side filter effects (e.g. dropping shadows), which you usually do not have when you work with vector graphics. SVG posseses an own filter element which allows you to apply one or more filters to an SVG object. Using this element you can blur an image, change its color saturation or characteristics, produce a beveled or embossed effect and lighting effects.

In addition to all those features SVG is also capable of applying different kinds of animation. The graphic designer has the tremendous possibility to transform or animate every single attribute or characteristic (e.g. position, colour, rotation, length, height,..) of his graphic. He can therefore make the graphic move around the screen, pop up from behind, rescale itself or react to different mouse events. A good and simple example of an animated SVG graphic written by Antoine Quint, who is the author of the XML.com   SVG   column,   can   be   viewed   at http://www.xml.com/2002/01/23/svg/cubes_final.svgz.

2 Implementations

Due to the fact that SVG is a rather young standard just a few programs dealing with SVG are currently available. A complete list of them can be found   at   http://www.w3.org/Graphics/SVG/SVG-Implementations.htm8. In my personal opinion Adobe and the open-source Apache XML project[6] are the most ambitious manufacturers of SVG software. They have both released a significant number of applications essential for the development and acceptance of SVG.

---

[6] More information about the Apache project can be found at http://xml.apache.org/

In the next two chapters I want to introduce you to the most developed and common SVG tools both for displaying SVG graphics and for creating your own SVG objects.

2.1 Displaying SVG

As I have already anticipated, only a small choice of SVG applications is publicly available at the moment. It is therefore obvious that all commonly used Internet browsers like Microsoft's Internet Explorer, Netscape's Navigator or Opera are unfortunately not able to display SVG graphics so far. Hence the user is forced to either install a browser plug-in or to use an application specially designed for presenting SVG objects.

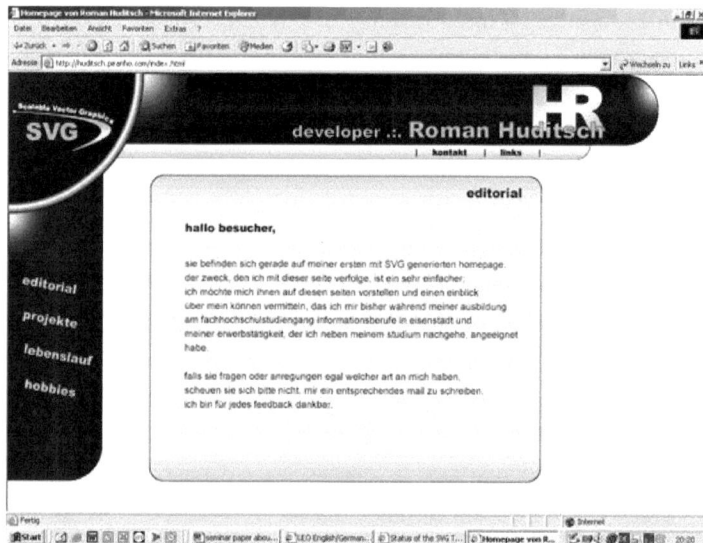

Image 2: Internet Explorer showing an SVG graphic with Adobe's SVG Viewer 3.0

The most comfortable option among those two possibilities is the one-time installation of an SVG plug-in. The most popular one is the SVG Viewer released by Adobe. The current version 3.0 is free for use and is available in more than 15 langauges. It can be downloaded at http://www.adobe.com/svg/viewer/install/main.html. Adobe has also participated actively in the development process of the SVG Recommendation and was one of its leading contributors. The first version of its viewing tool was even released in June, 2000, when SVG was still in its infancy. In comparison to other available SVG applications the SVG Viewer supports most parts of the SVG specification including the dynamic section of the SVG Recommendation, which contains scripting support, animations and transformations.

If you decide for a stand-alone SVG viewing application, you can either install the Batik SVG Toolkit developed by the Apache XML project, the CSIRO SVG Toolkit or the X-Smiles XML browser, which also supports other XML subsets like for example SMIL (Synchronized Multimedia Integration Language) or XForms.

The Batik SVG Toolkit "is a Java(tm) technology based toolkit for applications that want to use images in the Scalable Vector Graphics (SVG) format for various purposes, such as viewing, generation or manipulation." (Apache, 2001) The latest version of Batik (1.1) provides a complete support for all the static SVG features described in the specification and has has some rudimentary scripting support, too.

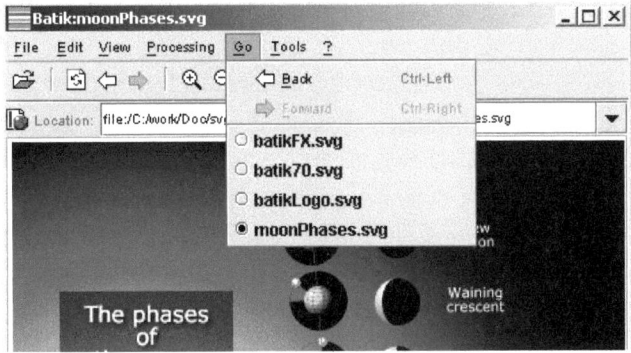

Image 3: Batik SVG Toolkit

Batik is an open- source project, which means that its source code can be viewed and complemented at any time. More detailed information about the current implementation status and the Batik SVG Toolkit in general can be found at http://xml.apache.org/batik/index.html.

Another option for stand-alone SVG viewing applications is the CSIRO SVG Toolkit, which is like Batik open- source software and therefore freely available. The current version of the toolkit was released on the 12th of March 2002. The SVG Toolkit contains an SVG viewer and utilities that make it possible to render an SVG document into various other image formats like JPG, PNG, TIFF or GIF. It is completely written in Java and therefore needs JDK 1.2 or higher for working. Although the application has problems rendering some of the SVG effects (e.g. blendings, Gaussion blurs or diffuse lighting), it provides a well developped scripting support. For further details about the CSIRO SVG Toolkit see its official website at http://sis.cmis.csiro.au/svg/.

An alternative to the Batik and CSIRO SVG Toolkit is the X-Smiles XML Browser developed in a non-profit project started by the Telecommunications Software and Multimedia Laboratory at Helsinki University of Technology. According to the official X-Smiles website (2000) "the main advantage of the X-Smiles browser is that it supports several XML related specifications and is still suitable for embedded devices supporting the Java environment." These supported XML specifications include XHTML, SMIL, XForms, XSLT (Extensible Stylesheet Language for Transformations), XSL-FO (XSL Formatting Objects) and of course SVG. The SVG implementation is realised by embedding the August 6th 2000 release of the CSIRO SVG Toolkit. Thus it appears that representing SVG objects is not X-Smiles primary purpose, but it is very qualified for showing the context (e.g. XHTML, XForms, SMIL) in which SVG can be embedded.

After describing the most commonly used tools for displaying SVG graphics, the subsequent chapter will deal with applications designed for creating them.

2.2   Tools for Creating SVG

Whereas the amount of SVG viewing applications is rather limited, there are a few more tools available for editing and converting SVG objects. Although you can create your SVG graphics with any common texteditor, it is far more easy to generate them with sophisticated drawing tools. In this chapter I want to provide you with some information about the most commonly used programs for this purpose. First of all it has to be mentioned that these programs can be divided into two main groups.

The first one includes all so-called native SVG editors, which are tools that have SVG as their primary file format and can read and modify SVG files without converting them to some other format. The most popular application among these native editors is Webdraw 1.0 developed by JASC. It offers most drawing- conveniences known from other graphic tools like Macromedia's Fireworks or Adobe's Photoshop.

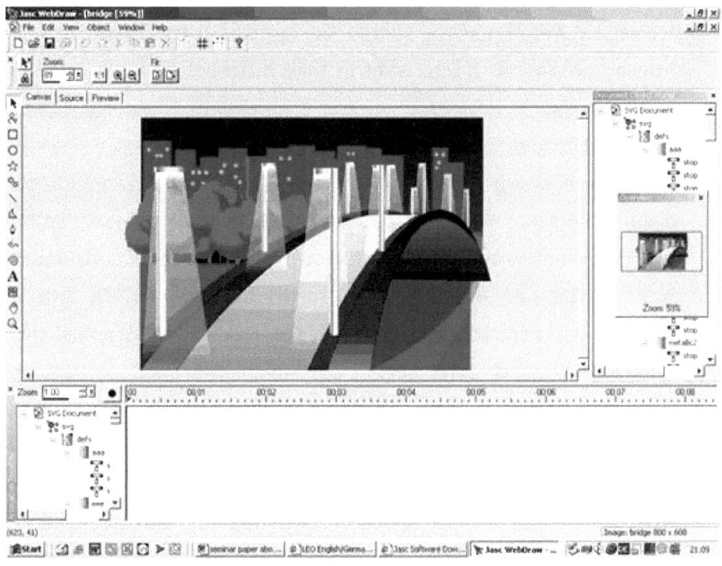

Image 4: Interface of JASC Webdraw 1.0

In addition to that the user is provided with a timeline for applying animations and for creating and editing keyframes. This animation concept was taken over from Macromedia's Flash and is therefore well- known by most of the users and easy to work with. Furthermore JASC Webraw offers you an extra window pane for viewing and writing SVG source code, which also allows you to automatically validate your written code. Even though SVG is Webdraw's basic file format, it can export your SVG objects to BMP or JPG graphics and it also supports SVGZ file compression, which means that you can additionally minimise the final file size. JASC Webdraw 1.0 is currently available for all Windows platforms for USD 129$, but you can also download a trial version which runs for 30 days.

Another interesting SVG tool is the open source project Sodipodi developed for Linux. Although it is still in early development – version 0.24.1 has been released recently - , many features have been implemented yet. For example both vector and bitmap objects can have alpha transparency and can be arbitrarily transformed. Like JASC Webdraw Sodipodi's user interface should be familiar from CorelDraw and similar drawing programs. If you want to take a deeper look into this application, you may download the needed source files at http://download.sourceforge.net/sodipodi/.

The second group of applications for creating SVG graphics contains all graphic programs which do not have SVG as their primary file format, but provide an ability to export SVG. However it has to be considered that this may exercise only a small portion of the features of SVG. Two of its most wide-spread exponents are the highly-developed graphic tools Adobe Illustrator 10 and Corel Draw! 10, which offer both import and export support for SVG. It is not possible to dwell on each of these products, because this would go beyond the scope of this seminar paper.

If you do not have the possibilities to use one of these tools, there are many small applications specially designed for converting SVG graphics into some other file format and vice versa. As I have mentioned before, SVG is provided with the same features as an ordinary Flash movie like being able to transform objects and doing other kinds of animations. Due to the similarity between these two formats it is not astonishing that a tool has been developed which is capable of transforming Flash movies into SVG graphics. Although this application, which was released by the University of Nottingham, is not publicaly available , it can be tried online at http://www.ep.cs.nott.ac.uk/~sgp/swf2svg.html.

If you need more information about such applications for generating SVG objects, you my find them at the official W3C website for SVG implementations[7] .

3 Conclusion

Although many SVG- specific applications are still in their infancy, there's no denying that SVG's importance regarding its involvement in Web design will increase continuously. Due to the fact that more and more applications are able to generate or work with SVG objects, Web designers do not have to face difficulties any longer when they want to create SVG graphics and embedded them in their websites. Almost unbounded possillites present themselves when you combine SVG graphics with other XML markup languages like XForms, which would allow you to transform your graphic, that may be for example a diagram, depending on any user input. If you want to know how this works in practice, you can visit the SVG demo site of Adobe[8] and see the "Chart and Graph" demo.

Even though this was rather a very general conspectus of the SVG's possililites and its current implementations, this seminar paper includes the most important points, which have to be mentioned regarding SVG, and provides clues where the interested reader can find further information about this new xml- based markup language for two-dimensional vector graphics.

---

[7] http://www.w3.org/Graphics/SVG/SVG-Implementations.htm8
[8] http://www.adobe.com/svg/demos/main.html

4 References

Apache XML project (2001). Batik SVG Toolkit.
Available: http://www.w3.org/TR/SVG/ [2002, March 22]

CSIRO Mathematical and Information Sciences (2002). CSIRO SVG
Toolkit. Available: http://sis.cmis.csiro.au/svg/ [2002, March 24]

Eisenberg, D. J.(2002). SVG Essentials. Cambridge: O'Reilly & Assoc.

Spona, H. (2001). Das Einsteigerseminar SVG – Webgrafiken mit XML.
Bonn: vmi- Buch AG.

Salathé, M. (2001). SVG- Scalable Vector Graphics. München: Markt &
Technik.

Quint; A. (2002). Digging Animation.
Available: http://www.xml.com/pub/a/2002/01/23/svg/index.html
[2002, March 13]

Quint; A. (2001). SVG: Where Are We Now?.
Available: http://www.xml.com/pub/a/2001/11/21/svgtools.html
[2002, March 13]

Watt, A. (2001). Designing SVG Web graphics: Visual components for
graphics in the Internet age. Indianapolis: New Riders Publishing.

World Wide Web consortium (2001). Scalable Vector Graphics (SVG)
1.0 Specification. Available: http://www.w3.org/TR/SVG/
[2002, March 13]

World Wide Web consortium (2002). Scalable Vector Graphics (SVG).
Available: http://www.w3.org/Graphics/SVG/ [2002, March 13]

World Wide Web consortium (1999). About the World Wide Web
consortium (W3C). Available: http://www.w3.org/Consortium/
[2002, March 17]

X-Smiles (2000). X-Smiles – an open xml browser for exotic devices.
Available: http://www.xsmiles.org/index.html
[2002, March 23]

5 Appendix

5.1 Glossary

Bitmap graphics   Bitmap or ratser formats treat each graphic as a collection of dots called bitmap, assigning a specific colour to each pixel. When viewed as a whole, this collection makes up an image.

Filter effects   "A filter effect consists of a series of graphics operations that are applied to a given source graphic to produce a modified graphical result." (W3C, 2001)

SMIL   "The Synchronized Multimedia Integration Language (SMIL, pronounced "smile") enables simple authoring of interactive audiovisual presentations. SMIL is typically used for "rich media"/multimedia presentations which integrate streaming audio and video with images, text or any other media type. SMIL is an easy-to-learn HTML-like language, and many SMIL presentations are written using a simple text-editor." (W3C, 2002)

SVG   SVG is the acronym for "Scalable Vector Graphics", which is a XML- based vector graphic standard for Web graphics developed by the World Wide Web consortium (W3C).

Vector graphics   Vector images are built up of many individual, scalable geometric objects defined by mathematical functions. Hence they consist of lines, curves, paths and other shapes. Therefore it is possible to render them at the highest feasible quality level.

W3C   "The World Wide Web Consortium was created in October 1994 to lead the World Wide Web to its full potential by developing common protocols that promote its evolution and ensure its interoperability. W3C has more than 500 Member organizations from around the world and has earned international recognition for its contributions to the growth of the Web." (W3C, 1999)

XForms   "XForms is an XML application that represents the next generation of Forms for the Web. By splitting traditional XHTML forms into three parts - data model, instance data, and user interface - it separates presentation from content, allows reuse, gives strong typing - reducing the number of round-trips to the server, as well as offering device independence and a reduced need for scripting.

XForms is not a free-standing document type, but is intended to be integrated into other markup languages, such as XHTML."

(W3C, 2002)

XHTML

"XHTML 1.0 is the W3C's first Recommendation for XHTML, following on from earlier work on HTML 4.01, HTML 4.0, HTML 3.2 and HTML 2.0. With a wealth of features, XHTML 1.0 is a reformulation of HTML 4.01 in XML, and combines the strength of HTML 4 with the power of XML.

XHTML 1.0 is the first major change to HTML since HTML 4.0 was released in 1997. It brings the rigor of XML to Web pages and is the keystone in W3C's work to create standards that provide richer Web pages on an ever increasing range of browser platforms including cell phones, televisions, cars, wallet sized wireless communicators, kiosks, and desktops."

(W3C, 2002)

XML

Stands for "Extensible Markup Language". XML was also developped by the W3C in 1996. More information can be found at http://www.w3.org/XML/

XSL-FO

With the help of XSL-FO stylesheets you can transform your XML document to any desired output format intended for printing like PostScript or PDF.

XSLT

XSLT is a markup language for transforming XML documents into other XML documents, HTML or WML documents or any other imaginable formats.